Wednesbury

IN OLD PHOTOGRAPHS

The town of Wednesbury began life as a small settlement within the precincts of an Iron Age hillfort we now know as Church Hill. This south-eastern view of about 1900 was taken on St George's Day, 23 April, made evident by the flag hoisted in St Bartholomew's churchyard. St Bartholomew's, the parish church, stands on the site of a heathen temple where the god Woden was once worshipped. Although much restored by the Victorians, there are still some good thirteenth- and fifteenth-century features to be seen. To the left, the Roman Catholic church of St Mary's was built in 1872 to the designs of Sir Gilbert Blount. The St Mary's church schools (centre) now serve as a social club. The Hall End shop, left foreground, was known as the 'Tommy shop', and was operated by the Quaker Lloyds family under the 'truck system', which meant wage payments of token coinage were exchangeable only there. The housing clustered around Ethelfelda Terrace, to the right, has all disappeared, while the houses provided for Patent Shaft employees in Hall End have not yet been built.

Wednesbury

IN OLD PHOTOGRAPHS

IAN M. BOTT

Budding
BOOKS

A Budding Book

First published in 1994 by Alan Sutton
Publishing Limited

This edition published in 1998 by Budding Books,
an imprint of Sutton Publishing Limited
Phoenix Mill · Thrupp · Stroud · Gloucestershire
GL5 2BU

A catalogue record for this book is available from
the British Library

ISBN 1-84015-081-5

Typesetting and origination by
Sutton Publishing Limited.
Printed in Great Britain by
WBC Limited, Bridgend, Mid-Glamorgan.

THE BLACK COUNTRY SOCIETY

This voluntary society, affiliated to the Civic Trust, was founded in 1967 as a reaction to the trend of the late 1950s and early 1960s to amalgamate everything into large units and in the Midlands to sweep away the area's industrial heritage in the process.

The general aim of the Society is to create interest in the past, present and future of the Black Country, and early on it campaigned for the establishment of an industrial museum. In 1975 the Black Country Museum was started by Dudley Borough Council on 26 acres of totally derelict land adjoining the grounds of Dudley Castle. This has developed into an award-winning museum which attracts over 250,000 visitors annually.

There are over two thousand members of the Black Country Society and all receive the quarterly magazine *The Blackcountryman*, of which over 105 issues have been published since its founding in 1967. In the whole collection there are some 1,500 authoritative articles on all aspects of the Black Country by historians, teachers, researchers, students, subject experts and ordinary folk with an extraordinary story to tell. The whole constitutes a unique resource about the area and is a mine of information for students and researchers who frequently refer to it. Many schools and libraries are subscribers. Three thousand copies of the magazine are printed each quarter. It is non-commercial, and contributors do not receive payment for their articles.

PO Box 71 · Kingswinford · West Midlands DY6 9YN

Contents

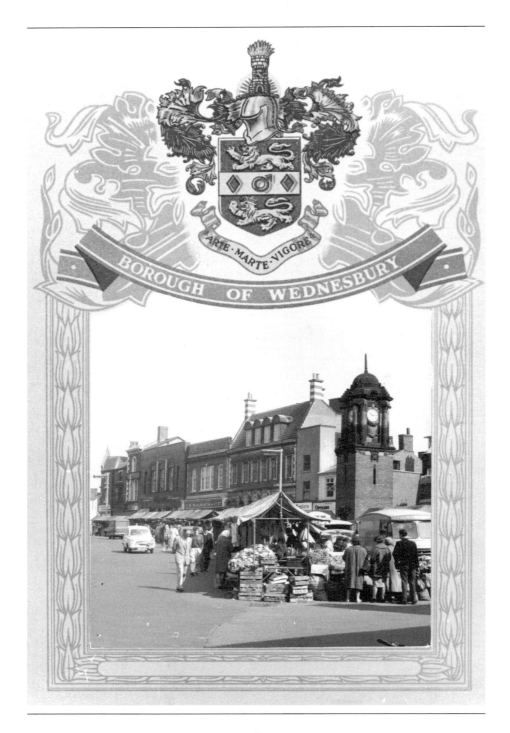

ARTE · MARTE · VIGORE

BOROUGH OF WEDNESBURY

Introduction

The latin *arte marte vigore* from the former Wednesbury Corporation's 1904 coat of arms (pictured opposite with a 1960s view of Market Place) was a fitting motto for this stronghold of industry: translated it means 'by skill, by iron, by energy'.

Indeed, Wednesbury was founded as a stronghold in the Iron Age hillfort – traces of which still ring the ancient Church Hill – its name derived from Wodon, the Saxon god of war. It is this site which became one of Princess Ethelfelda's chain of Mercian strongholds in AD 916, she being the daughter of King Alfred the Great.

The 'Wadnesberie' of Domesday Book was, in 1086, a thriving rural community, encompassing Bloxwich and Shelfield, now parts of the modern borough of Walsall. Originally the Manor of Wednesbury was Crown property, until Henry II exchanged it with the Heronville family, for the town of Stuntsfield, in Oxfordshire. Thus it has passed through many great English families to the present-day lords of the manor – the Foleys.

Wednesbury's most famous son must have been William Paget. Born in 1505, the son of a nailer, he rose to be Secretary of State to King Henry VIII, and later became the 1st Marquis of Anglesey.

The town's most recalled episode in history is the treatment of the Revd John Wesley during the anti-Methodist riots of 1743, in which he almost lost his life (see pages 88 and 89). It is true that Wednesbury had its fair share of hell-raisers in the eighteenth century. The last verse of the celebrated chant 'Wedgbury Cocking' declares that 'they are all savage by nature and guilty of deeds most shocking'! Yet it was also these people who helped Wednesbury prosper, toiling in the unearthly conditions of the collieries and furnaces.

It was the Industrial Revolution that was to change the face of Wednesbury for ever. Although 'cole pits' are recorded as early as 1315, it was not until the advent of the modern age that large-scale exploitation of the area's minerals began. Recent archaeological excavations have revealed that clay was an early extraction, for use in a widespread pottery making industry producing 'Wedgbury-ware'. However, the presence also of iron ore and limestone, in addition to coal, provided the three main ingredients for iron making.

The first ironworks sprang up on the banks of the River Tame and its tributaries, employing the water wheel to provide the necessary power. Wednesbury Forge is mentioned as early as 1597 and is still a centre of edge-tool making today. Later, many factories straddled the canal banks, taking advantage of the cheap and direct transport they offered. Wednesbury's first canal was cut in 1769 to connect the town's coalfields with the industries of Birmingham.

Other industries prevalent in eighteenth-century Wednesbury included enamelling and gun-barrel forging. The latter became the town's chief industry for over one hundred years, when its products were adapted to provide gas tubing. Wednesbury became generally known as 'Tubetown' in far-off places.

It was Cornelius Whitehouse (1795–1883), an Oldbury man who settled in Wednesbury, who brought about great changes to the tube industry with his 1825 patent for the 'butt-welded tube', while engaged with James Russell's Crown Tube Works. His improvement consisted of drawing the folded and heated tube through a conical die, so that it automatically welded at the joint when passed from the broader to the narrower end of the hole. Although his invention earned him royalties of £500 per year, Whitehouse became the subject of much hostility from barrel forgers, who now found themselves robbed of a trade. Later, he went on to found his own 'Globe Tube Works' at Holloway Bank.

The versatility of iron, coupled with the constant inventions and innovations of the new Victorian age, led to ironworks springing up all over Wednesbury, producing everything from holloware to cast-iron bridges. With this came the dramatic rise in population as people flocked in from all over the country to fill the thousands of vacancies created.

Of all the many ironworks established during this boom-time, one rose to become Wednesbury's greatest employer, outliving many of its competitors. The Patent Shaft and Axletree Company was established in 1834 by the Revd James Hardy, a Baptist minister in the town. Operating from the vast Brunswick, Monway and Old Park works, in 1959 it became known as the Patent Shaft Steelworks. The townsfolk reeled in 1980 at the news of its closure.

Another once great concern in the town was F.H. Lloyd and Company, Steelworks. It was Sampson Lloyd II (1699–1779) who established this Welsh Quaker family's links with the town, marrying Sarah, the daughter of Richard Parkes, a Wednesbury ironmaster. It was he also who became co-founder of the famous Lloyd's banking empire.

Communications with Wednesbury were much enhanced by Thomas Telford's 1826 improvements to the London to Holyhead coach road. The 1783 Walsall Canal, running north-east, was joined in 1844 with the Tame Valley Canal, skirting the southern extremity of the town. The Grand Junction Railway arrived at Wood Green in 1837, followed by the London and North Western and Great Western lines in 1850 and 1854 respectively.

Wednesbury's Charter of Incorporation, granted by Queen Victoria in 1886, led to many social improvements, including better sanitation and the provision of public buildings. Housing among the working classes remained poor until slum clearance programmes were effected between the wars.

In 1961 Wednesbury celebrated the seventy-fifth anniversary of its Incorporation. However, its centenary celebrations were not to be realized, for in 1966 it became part of the County Borough of West Bromwich, which in turn became part of the Metropolitan Borough of Sandwell in 1974.

SECTION ONE

Shops and Stalls

Mary Greenhough is joined by four of her grandchildren, at the family business B. Greenhough, bakers, at 45 Holyhead Road, in 1916.

William Jones' tobacconists, 77 Holyhead Road, which ran a sideline in moneylending, *c.* 1910. Strangely, No. 78 next door was a pawnbroker also named Jones, although no relation.

Mr Alfred Stiles ran his furnishings business from these Walsall Street premises, pictured about 1910. Note the children's high chairs displayed on the right.

Established in 1857, Henry Hollingsworth Pork Butcher moved to these purpose-built premises at 82 Holyhead Road in 1879. Pictured in 1906, they boasted steam-powered apparatus.

The Union Hardware Company displays an extensive array of galvanized ware at 70 Union Street in 1916.

John Price Newsagents decked up for carnival day, 11 September 1926. Miss Lilian Greenhough, dressed in pierrot outfit, is joined by customers at the 48 Holyhead Road premises.

Seven gas lamps were installed to illuminate the pavement display of Sidney Jowett's Poulterers and Fruiterers at 1 Walsall Street, photographed c. 1920.

Pictured in 1916, S.R. Poxon, Furnisher, of 20 and 21 Lower High Street. Also sold were wringing machines, mail carts, pianos, bicycles and antiques.

A good example of self-advertisement is evident in this picture of Thomas Purslow's Bakers, at 42 Bridge Street, 1906. After winning prize medals for pork pie making in 1912 and 1913, they built their Prize Medal Bakery in New Street in 1920.

Shop assistant Miss Florrie Wedgbury
at Edith Minett's Ladies Outfitters,
83 Walsall Street, *c*. 1940.

J. Byrne Tailors began and finished trading
from premises in Lower High Street.
In between they occupied this Holloway
Bank building, which was demolished
in September 1986.

E. Austin, Leather Dealers, was founded at 54 Union Street by Edwin Austin, JP, who lived in Wharfdale Street, and ran the business with his brothers. Later, the concern was purchased by George J. Dale, who made his home at Portland House, Wood Green. Pictured here in around 1928 are, left to right: David Knowles, George J. Dale, Ernest John Randle, Gladys Timmins, Nellie Pratt, Joseph Pratt. The premises were demolished in January 1993 to make way for a supermarket development.

Wednesbury's singing barber, the late Toni Amorosa (senior) stands in the doorway to his salon, 33 Upper High Street, in 1966. Later the business was continued in Union Street until 1987.

Nicholls Newsagents traded from converted cottage premises at 73 Lower High Street, now demolished. Only the White Horse Hotel of 1846 remains from this view of 1968.

Watchmaker and jeweller Marian Maczka proudly stands alongside his Christmas window display at 49 Union Street in December 1955. Founded in Dudley Street in 1952, the business traded at a further two Union Street sites before changing hands in 1986.

Nos 1 to 5 Market Place, 1986. They became the site of an archaeological survey after demolition in February 1989. Archaeologists uncovered an eighteenth-century pottery kiln on the spot where the town Job Centre was built in 1993.

Photographed in February 1987 are 13 to 22 Walsall Street, which succumbed to the bulldozer in 1990. The shop on the far right was one of two branches of Jackson's Chemists.

'Wedgbury Market', *c.* 1900. This was established from Queen Anne's Royal Charter of 1709, and so is one of the oldest in the Black Country. The triple-headed gas lamp occupied the site of the Market Cross building, which was erected in 1709 and demolished in 1824. Wedgbury is the seventeenth-century version of the town's name.

Labour party members campaigning at their propaganda stall, February 1959.

Bargain hunters examine the merchandise in this busy 1968 scene. Market days have long been held on Fridays and Saturdays.

In 1970 the market was moved to a canopied site in nearby Camp Street, seen here in 1971. Later the open sides were replaced with brick walls.

SECTION TWO

Schooldays

A snow scene lies before the children of Standard I at Mesty Croft Junior School in 1912. One wonders whether it was wintertime or a geography lesson!

Group 5 girls gather for the photographer in their 'best whites', at St James' National Schools, *c.* 1910. This is now Wednesbury's oldest surviving school building, dating back to 1845.

Lower High Street Board Schools, Standard V, line up in front of the 'undercroft', *c.* 1907. A full view of these buildings can be seen on page 28.

Infants learn about shopping at St Bartholomew's Schools, 1939. The five girls to the left have their pennies ready to purchase bottled milk.

The Albert Pritchard Memorial School was newly built when this photograph was taken outside the nursery section in 1939. This Crew Road school was named after Sir Albert Pritchard, six times mayor of the town.

Open-air dancing at St Bartholomew's Schools, 1939. This was the first church school in the town, erected in 1829. The couple centre background appear to have fallen out!

Another dancing class, 1939. This time, pupils join in folk dancing at Mesty Croft Schools in Alma Street.

Kings Hill, Standard VI, *c.* 1916. These Board Schools of 1887 were destroyed in a fierce blaze in 1992.

Holyhead Road senior girls learn cookery skills, 1939. Ingredients had to be cheap and came in short measure because of war rationing.

Senior girls take physical training in the yard of Holyhead Road Schools, 1939. Notice how they are synchronized for the camera.

Headmaster Sidney Foote lines up with Kings Hill Seniors football team, who proudly display their trophies, c. 1935.

Senior boys learn to use the forge, 1939. 'Metal bashing' was an important skill to learn in what was then an important centre of steel making.

Senior girls create a school garden at Holyhead Road, 1939. The classrooms pictured behind the boundary wall occupied the site of the Archer Close housing development. The roller looks formidable and takes two girls to push it.

Mountford Primary School staged an Elizabethan pageant to celebrate the coronation of HRH Queen Elizabeth II, June 1953.

Lower High Street Board Schools were built in 1880, but twice changed names before demolition, taking place in this 1980 picture. After a spell as Mountford Primary School, they became known as St John's Church of England Schools, replacing the Russell Street Schools of the same name in 1964.

Stern headmaster C.H.S. Kipping joins this gathering of masters and pupils at Wednesbury Boys' High School, 1928. This establishment was set up in 1924 at Wood Green Lodge, St Paul's Road, the former home of the Pritchard family of tube founders. Here, before the Second World War, the game of chess was introduced to the pupils, culminating with the winning of the British Chess Federation Shield in 1939. However, C.H.S. Kipping is better remembered for his open-air classes, held in sun, rain and snow. The masters pictured front row, left to right, are: W.R. Swale, P.R. Hatcher, A.C. Evanson, C.H.S. Kipping, R.V. Rutherford, W.R. Hey, F. Coatham and Sergeant Allerston.

Wednesbury Boys' High School, 1932. Seen to the left is the original Wood Green Lodge, while far right is the assembly hall added in 1926, with the central portion of 1932. Wood Green Lodge was demolished in 1960 and the remainder of the buildings were absorbed into Wood Green High School.

The tennis courts at Wednesbury Boys' High School, 1933. Boys who wished to play had to provide their own racquets.

SECTION THREE
In the Workplace

Employees of Hubert John Barlow's Mounts Works, situated off Bridge Street, 1928. In addition to bright drawn steels, Mr Barlow also produced bricks, and owned the Wednesbury Hippodrome in Upper High Street.

Miners at the Blue Fly Colliery prepare to descend in the cage, 1897. No safety barriers are evident. Only a sling chain is provided to hold on to.

Wednesbury colliers returning from work, 1897. 'Cole pits' were mentioned at Wednesbury as far back as 1315. The town lies on the famous 10-yd South Staffordshire coal seam.

William Charles owned Wednesbury Bridge New Coal Wharf on the Tame Valley Canal, seen here in 1897. The company advertised coals including 'cobbles, Staffordshire thick and fine slack'.

Work meets work in this turn-of-the-century picture of sewer laying alongside James Russell's Crown Tube Works in High Bullen. Russell's produced steel tubing for the gas industry.

JOHN BAGNALL & SONS LIMITED,

Leabrook Ironworks, Wednesbury

London Office:
8, Laurence
Pountney Hill,
E.C.

Telegrams:
"Bagnall,
Wednesbury."

Telephone:
24, Wednesbury.

John Bagnall's Leabrook Ironworks, pictured in 1906, were built alongside the Walsall canal before 1800, where they stood until demolition in 1992.

The interior of Robert Ryder's Wharfdale printing works, 1897. In these premises, gas-powered machinery produced the *Wednesbury Herald*, Ryder's Annuals and picture postcards.

Staff of the Smithy Department, Old Park Works, c. 1910. They were part of the massive Patent Shaft and Axletree Company, which was a major employer in the town.

Patent Shaft and Axletree Company offices, Leabrook Road, seen here newly built in 1901. Besides the Old Park Works, the company also ran the Brunswick and Monway plants.

William Jones, one of the last shinglers, wears his amazing leg 'armour', which gave protection against white-hot sparks when hammering pig iron into wrought iron.

The heat can almost be felt in this picture of the Patent Shaft interior, 1968. In the distance on the left can be seen the tank-like furnace charger.

Patent Shaft workers break from production, 1968. The works, which were founded in 1834, closed in 1980, and were finally demolished in 1986.

A reminder that Wednesbury was once in a rural setting is given in this picture of milking time, Hobbs Hole Farm, Wood Green, 1913. Standing in the centre is Luke Rowland, with Edwin Banner on the right.

Pictured in 1923 with son, Alec (left), is Alfred Horace Nicholls (1871–1945), who ran a mangle sales and coachbuilding business at 15 Holyhead Road.

William Mills Aluminium Foundry, Friar Park Road, 1962. The founder of the works invented the Mills grenade during the Second World War.

Interior of the William Mills foundry, *c.* 1960. During the Second World War, the foundry served as a 'shadow' factory, producing munitions under a cloak of secrecy.

Brinton, Adams and Richards, Potters Lane, 1968. This company started life as Edward Smith's Brunswick Tube Works in 1850.

The Village Walk housing complex now stands on the site of Thomas Pritchard's South Staffordshire Tube Works, built in 1856 and photographed in 1968.

This advertisement of 1956 features two of William Sanders' electrical products made at the company's Ridding Lane works.

William Sanders Falcon Electrical Works later became known as the Ottermill. The Gregory Close housing development now occupies the site, pictured during demolition in September 1987.

Founded in 1893, Hickinbottom's advertised their bread with the slogan 'Mother likes it, so do I'. Pictured in 1930 is a section of the Electric Bakery, Stafford Street, which was demolished in May 1992.

Wednesbury and Walsall postmen gather at the District Head Office for this presentation, c. 1960.

Workers are seen hot-dipping galvanized window frames at Henry Hope and Sons, Woden Road West, 1963. The tank contained 120 tons of zinc maintained at 852°F.

Roy Millward, relief projectionist, changes the film reel at the Odeon, Walsall Street, 1970. Built as the Gaumont, it later changed its name to the Odeon, before becoming the Silver.

An aerial view of Wednesbury Forge, 1960. It shows the industrial site first mentioned in 1597 and taken over by Edward Elwell in 1817.

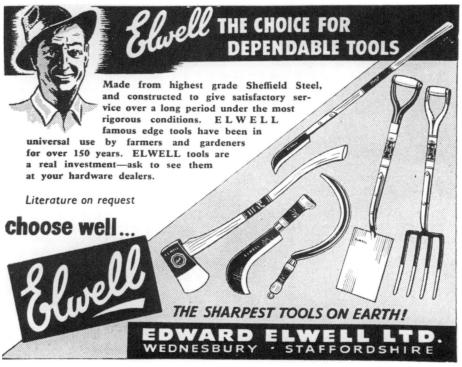

Elwell's claimed to make 'the sharpest tools on earth', as this 1968 advertisement states.

Testing shovels at Edward Elwell's, 1960. If the head did not spring back into shape when bent, the tool was rejected.

Office workers from the Ega Tube Company in Holyhead Road take a break in the summer sunshine of 1963.

George Croft's Bright Drawn Steels was the last surviving remnant of James Russell's Crown Tube Works. The High Bullen factory, pictured in 1968, was demolished in 1989.

SECTION FOUR

Leisure Hours

This young Wednesbury family is probably setting out on a Sunday treat. The picture was taken in Brunswick Park Road at the turn of the century.

Six members of the Jones family, tobacconists at 77 Holyhead Road, enjoy their pipes in this early studio picture.

Neighbours from Little Hill take a break in the rural Delves district, 1924. This area is a few miles south-east of the town centre and was part of Wednesbury until the 1930s. Sarah Geraghty is far left, while Frances Turton is second from the right.

Brunswick Park was opened in 1887 to commemorate Queen Victoria's Golden Jubilee. Here, the Park Lodge entrance is seen in 1910. The park was created by Messrs Baron and Son of Derby on 28 acres of waste land purchased from the Patent Shaft and Axletree Co. for £3,000.

The Invalids' Walk, Brunswick Park, *c.* 1912. It was so named because of its gentle climb with plenty of seating.

This 1951 photograph shows, left to right: Ethel Price, Mrs R. Copeland, Jean Lovatt and Sheila Marston (attendants), Gillian Scott (Carnival Queen), Mayor Leonard Whitehouse, Lord Burdon CBE, Mrs L. Whitehouse.

Contestants for the dog show square up at Brunswick Park, 1950.

Miss Wedgbury and Miss Minett are seen playing on the Russian cannon, *c.* 1935. The gun was captured during the Crimean War in 1854 and later placed in Brunswick Park.

Charles Southern JP presented the children's drinking fountain to the town's Brunswick Park in 1889. Sadly it disappeared during the Second World War.

Workers from William Plimley's Carriage Works, Red Lion Mews, Bridge Street, on an outing to the Fighting Cocks Inn, near Wolverhampton, *c.* 1905.

The Essanay Film Company sent this Red Indian horseman to advertise a forthcoming film in the Market Place in 1913.

Kings Hill Park was opened on what had been a colliery mound in 1900. Here, residents relax in its surroundings in about 1911.

These Wednesbury gentlemen are in the Anchor Hotel yard, Holyhead Road, *c.* 1933. Opposite can be seen the old cottages which occupied the site of Russell House flats.

Turkeys and beef joints were the Christmas Draw prizes at the Civil Defence Club, Hawthorne Road, in 1971.

Brothers Eric and Alan Bott at play in George Street, 1941. This street was cleared during the 1960s and now provides a small unofficial car park off Loxdale Street.

Hill Top Cycling Club pictured in Holloway Bank at the start of their 'Hobo run' to Kinver, 1951. Holloway Bank forms the border between Wednesbury and West Bromwich.

Former mayor, David Chadwick Jackson, conducts the Town Hall Orchestra, c. 1964.

Party time for residents of The Oval, toasting the marriage of Prince Charles to Lady Diana Spencer, 1981.

SECTION FIVE
War and Peace

Wednesbury Boer War soldiers pictured on their safe return, 1902. Lieutenant Smith is seated centre, with, left to right: S. Silk, W. Wiseman, R. Ward, W. Moseley, J. Farmer, T. Pym, A.J. Williams, A. Banks, bugler Farnsworth, J. Severn.

Wednesbury Volunteer Sergeants, 1908. Back row, left to right: A.H. Webb, F. Pym, F.N. Bodin, H.H. Smith, F.E. Harrison, R. Ward, F. Elsmore. Middle row: J. Eyre, J. Wakelam, W.E. Booth, W.E. Farley, G. Cox. Front row: A. Collett, H. Noakes, J. Gregg.

Locals gather to watch a parade of the 5th Battalion, South Staffordshire Regiment, at the Drill Hall, Bridge Street, 1908.

Wednesbury soldiers are among this group of 'Staffords', pictured during the First World War.

Management and staff from the munitions department at Samuel Platt's Kings Hill Foundry, 1915.

Mesty Croft Peace Treat was held every August Bank Holiday to celebrate the end of the First World War. Here, the procession halts at the Village Inn, Alma Street, in about 1921.

Sir Ian Hamilton, Commander in Chief of the 'Staffords' is pictured (centre) officiating at the dedication of the War Memorial, Walsall Street, in 1926.

Council officials and the Military make their speeches at the War Relief fundraising stand in Oakeswell End, during 1942.

The country's first purpose-built shell production plant opened at Stewart and Lloyd's New Crown works in 1938. King George VI made this inspection visit on 26 October 1939.

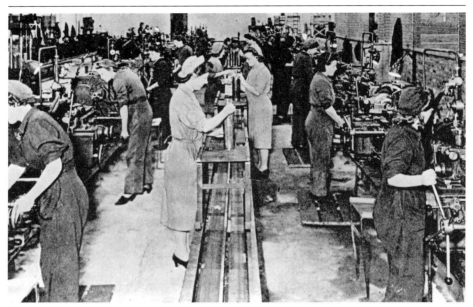

Women munition workers turned out 18,000 anti-aircraft shells per week at the Bilport Lane plant.

A woman munitions worker operates a machine, riveting base plates to shell cases. Most women who were employed during the war had never been in a factory before.

VE Day 1945 was celebrated with toffee apples by the Price and Small families of Myvod Road. The women hold up their treats while the children tuck in immediately.

Eagles' shop provides the backdrop for the Paul Street VE Day party. Some children attended in fancy dress.

A bonfire followed this Hamstead Terrace street party which, despite rationing, provided quite a luxurious spread.

Until the Fire Brigade assumed the responsibility of civil defence duties, the voluntary Civil Defence Movement continued to stage mock evacuation exercises in post-war Britain. Pictured is such an event outside the Cottage Spring, at the junction of Bilston Road and Darlaston Road, in about 1950.

Wednesbury's 'A Team' stretcher another 'casualty' to their field ambulance.

Wednesbury Civil Defence Volunteers women's section, pictured with their new minibus, 1962. Left to right: Katharine Clark, Elsie Russell, Rene Russell, -?-, Hilda Proctor.

Leslie Crouch fits Albert Russell with a gas mask, watched by fellow civil defence volunteers, c. 1955.

SECTION SIX

Sports

Wednesbury Old Athletic football team, March 1877. Back row, left to right: N. Fellows, J. Rotton, W. Moon, W. Dickinson, G. Skidmore, H. Willies. Middle row: C.A. Hatfield, S. Page, J.W. Knight, W.H. Johnson, J. Stokes. Front row: E. Holmes, J. Page, J. Reeves.

The Wednesbury Wood Green football team, probably at the Cottage Inn, Wood Green, 1906.

Wednesbury Tennis Club, seen here in 1911, had four courts at its disposal, adjoining the town's cricket ground at Wood Green. Their headquarters were at the Horse and Jockey.

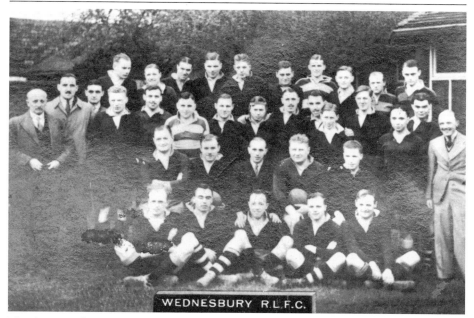

This line-up of Wednesbury Rugby League Football Club in the 1930s included many of its 1921 founder members, such as Percy Clifford (second left) and David Chadwick ('Chad') Jackson (centre).

'Chad' Jackson (with camera) joins the now renamed Wednesbury Rugby Union Football Club at their Hydes Road pitch, 1954.

Members of Wednesbury Golf Club relax at the clubhouse, Holden Road, 1927. When the 5,502-yd nine hole course closed after the Second World War, the building was removed to Quatford as a holiday chalet.

Wednesbury Cricket Club players, *c.* 1957. Their 'Oval' ground at Wood Green became part of Wednesbury Sports Union in 1936.

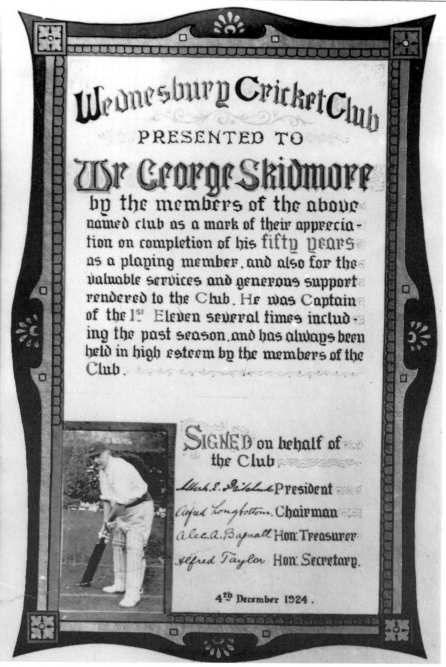

Wednesbury Cricket Club

PRESENTED TO

Mr George Skidmore

by the members of the above named club as a mark of their appreciation on completion of his fifty years as a playing member, and also for the valuable services and generous support rendered to the Club. He was Captain of the 1st Eleven several times including the past season, and has always been held in high esteem by the members of the Club.

SIGNED on behalf of the Club

Albert E. Pritchard President

Alfred Longbottom. Chairman

Alec A. Bagnall Hon. Treasurer

Alfred Taylor Hon. Secretary.

4th December 1924.

Illuminated address to George Skidmore. Born in 1854, he played his first match aged ten.

The FA Cup (won by West Bromwich Albion) and the Football League Championship Cup (won by Wolverhampton Wanderers) were photographed with Tony Mallam (centre) at Kings Hill Fields in 1954.

Wednesbury Midland Electricity Board employees play comic football in 1958, at their Bayleys Lane, Ocker Hill, sports ground.

SECTION SEVEN

Mayor's Parlour

The Mayor, Councillor Edwin James Hunt JP is seen, joined by Town Hall colleagues, at the dedication of the George V coronation clock tower on 9 November 1911. A picture of the earlier foundation stone-laying ceremony appears on page 76.

Alderman Richard Williams JP, a native of Liverpool, became Wednesbury's first mayor 1886–8. Residing at Brunswick House, 57 Holyhead Road, he was Managing Director of the Patent Shaft and Axletree Company.

Alderman Sir Albert Pritchard JP (1859–1937) was six times mayor of the town between 1901 and 1921. The son of tube founder Thomas Pritchard, he was knighted in 1923.

Alderman John Ashly Kilvert JP served as Mayor in 1905–6. A veteran of the Crimean War, he was nursed back to health by Florence Nightingale, following the Charge of the Light Brigade. On his death in 1920, he left his sword and medals to the corporation.

Alderman John Handley JP, Mayor in 1906–8, gave the site of the public library, and he and his sister, Jane, donated granite horse troughs in 1905 and 1910 respectively. The troughs can still be seen in Union Street.

Councillor Edwin James Hunt JP lays the foundation stone of the George V Coronation clock tower in Market Place, 22 June 1911. The clock, with its four 3-ft diameter dials, is controlled from the Town Hall and originally chimed each hour.

This 1942 mayoral parade passes Spring Head Villas in Walsall Street. The mayor (centre) is Councillor David Chadwick Jackson.

Mayor and Mayoress Councillor and Mrs D.C. Jackson, pictured in their second term of office, 1943–4. The mayor's robes were presented by Alderman Wilson Lloyd JP in 1900. The mayoral chains, presented in 1886 and 1901 respectively, were stolen during a raid on West Bromwich Town Hall in the 1970s.

Alderman Leonard Whitehouse JP proclaims Elizabeth II queen outside the Town Hall, 1952. The mace, held by Bruce Bennett, was given by Alderman Richard Williams JP in 1886.

The mayor, Councillor J.F. Postins JP, presides over a meeting in the council chamber, 1953.

The mayor, Councillor J.F. Postins JP (centre) attending the Wednesbury Horticultural Show, Brunswick Park, 1953.

Wednesbury's seventy-fifth anniversary charter celebrations gala was held at Hydes Road playing fields on 8 July 1961. The mayor, Councillor Leonard Waldron, carves from the 120 lb pig roast.

Joining the line-up with Councillor Mark Allen, mayor 1963–4, is Mr John Stonehouse (centre), Wednesbury's then MP.

Electoral officer, Mr Leslie Crouch, sits to the left of Mr and Mrs Arthur Rawlings – last Mayor and Mayoress of Wednesbury – at the Civil Defence Club, 1965.

SECTION EIGHT

Religion

St Bartholomew's parish church is shown here in its medieval form, before Victorian restoration, in a drawing by the Revd Stebbing Shaw dating from 1798.

Interior of St Bartholomew's, *c.* 1880, before the great restoration of 1885. The three-decker pulpit, dated 1611, stands in its original form, as does the alabaster monument to Richard and Dorothy Parkes, dated 1628, which was removed from the chancel to the south-west door. The church contains fifteen stained glass windows by Charles Eamer Kempe MA.

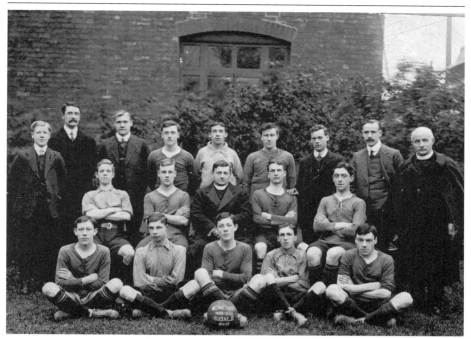

Wednesbury Parish Church 'Social II' FC, at their Brunswick Terrace headquarters, 1912.

Twelve activity rooms and a neat bowling green were provided at Wednesbury YMCA, opened in 1903 at 52 Lower High Street. The gardens are seen here in 1905.

St Luke's Mission Church, Alma Street, Mesty Croft, began life in 1874 as a charity school. Rebuilt in 1885, it was demolished and replaced in the 1970s.

This delightful view of Wood Green Road in 1905 shows St Paul's Church, built by the Elwell family of Wednesbury Forge in 1874. The churchyard wall is capped with quartered millstones.

St James' Church was built of stone quarried from Monway Field in 1847. This centenary gathering of 1947 shows the building where 'Sister Dora' – Walsall nurse Dorothy Pattison – chose to worship.

Side by side, the Congregational church of 1848, Russell Street, and St John's, Lower High Street, built 1846. Seen from Holyhead Road in 1968, the former is now the Masonic Hall, while the latter was demolished in July 1985.

Mesty Croft's Elwell Street Methodist Sunday school choir is pictured in Red House grounds, June 1927.

Formerly Church Hill House, the residence of George Silas Guy JP, St Mary's convent day school is seen here in 1953. Nos 56–74 Church Hill now occupy the site.

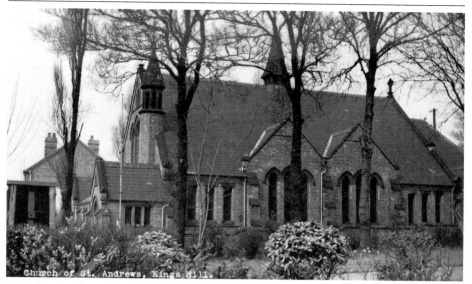

St Andrew's Church, seen from the adjoining Kings Hill Park, *c.* 1950. The church was dedicated in 1894.

Players in this production of *Paul's Dream* line up for the camera at the Baptist church, Holyhead Road, 1953.

Wednesbury is infamous for the shocking treatment meted out to the Revd John Wesley (1704–91) by its townspeople, on the evening of 20 October 1743. While Wesley was staying at the Bridge Street home of Francis Ward, a colliery manager, the anti-Methodist mob, incited by the Revd Edward Egginton of the parish church, arrived to convey the founder of Methodism to the magistrate Colonel Lane, at Bentley Hall, 2 miles distant. However, on arrival at the hall, they were turned away by Colonel Lane's son, being told to 'go home and be quiet'! Undeterred, the mob made their way to Justice Persehouse's residence in Walsall, where they received a similar reply. Resigned to return to Wednesbury, they were suddenly surprised and overpowered by the rival Walsall mob. In the chaos that ensued, Wesley made his escape from his persecuters, assisted by 'Honest Munchin', real name George Clifton, and four others: William Sitch, Edward Slater, John Griffiths and Joan Parks. Above is a nineteenth-century interpretation of the events by Marshall Claxton RA.

Pictured in their original position, giving access to a malt-house along High Bullen, these steps were often used by John Wesley as a pulpit. Removed in 1891, they now stand beside the Central Mission in Spring Head.

'Honest Munchin's' cottage, Holloway Bank, 1903. George Clifton 1704–89 was a collier and prize-fighter, who later took to preaching the gospel. The cottage, marked with an X, was demolished in 1934.

A full house seems evident for this meeting of Central Methodist Youth Club at Spring Head Schools, 1954.

Spring Head Central Methodist Church, built in 1867 and demolished in 1965, is seen here in 1954.

SECTION NINE

Pub Crawl

The Talbot Hotel, 27 Market Place, *c.* 1910. It was built in 1879 for John Taylor Duce and sons, wine merchants, replacing an Elizabethan inn. (See also pages 105 and 108.)

Two buglers sit among the eighteen passengers of the Mayflower. This very rare picture of the Sampson and Lion, High Bullen, dates from around 1895.

Ye Olde Leathern Bottel, Vicarage Road, 1899. It is reputed to have been built in 1510 and patronized by Dick Turpin, the infamous highwayman.

Taking its name from the nearby railway, the London and North Western Hotel, pictured *c.* 1938, stood on the corner of Stafford Street and Albert Street.

A family gathering at the rear of the Foresters Arms, Oxford Street, 1890. Back row, left to right: Emmy Rowley, Jack Heywood, David Heywood, Ben Heywood, Bill Heywood, Lottie Willets. Front row: Sam Heywood, Charlotte Heywood, Jim Heywood.

Regulars of the Old Barrel, Darlaston Road, Kings Hill, lined up for this picture in the 1920s before setting off on a charabanc ride.

The Plough and Harrow, 58 Leabrook Road, was frequented by thirsty steel workers – as it was next to the entrance gates of the Patent Shaft Steelworks.

Licensee Richard Henry Collett stands with a child outside the Three Tuns, 58 Union Street, 1936.

The Stores, 1968. It stood in Holyhead Road at its busy junction with Dudley Street.

The Red Lion, Bridge Street. Believed to be the hostelry pictured in the Wednesbury Riots (see page 88), it was demolished in March 1983.

The Nag's Head, Lower High Street, 1968. It had bricked-up windows, a reminder of the eighteenth-century window tax.

Named after the adjoining tube works, the Globe Inn, Holloway Bank, was demolished in the 1970s.

The Foresters Arms, Oxford Street, 1968. This was one of several Mesty Croft hostelries closed in the 1960s and 1970s.

Customers gather for a sing-song around the piano for this delightful picture, taken at the Old Barrel, Darlaston Road, Kings Hill, in 1955.

Benjamin and Eliza Nicholls built the Prince Regent piecemeal in the 1860s. The Victoria Street pub is pictured in 1968.

Wednesbury Market now occupies the site of the Jolly Brewer, Camp Street, seen here alongside the Primitive Methodist chapel of 1824. Both were demolished in 1970.

Licensee Frederick Mitchell washes glasses behind the bar of the Dog and Partridge, Ridding Lane, December 1962.

The Castle Inn, 1968. It was a solidly built Georgian hostelry, which stood on the corner of Walsall Street and Windmill Street until demolition, *c.* 1978.

Mesty Croft's Museum Inn, Elwell Street, seen here in 1968, not long before its demolition.

Dog and Partridge licensee Frederick Mitchell is seen again, this time having a 'night off' to join customers in the smoke room, 1968.

The Swan Inn, Moxley Road, 1986. When it was pulled down in November 1989, an unfilled mineshaft was discovered in the yard.

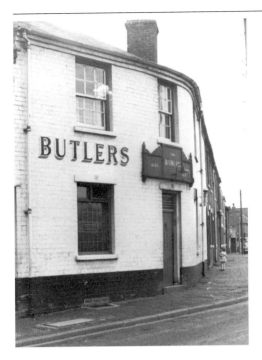

The Rising Sun, 114 Piercy Street, 1965. It is another of Mesty Croft's public houses that has disappeared.

The Great Western Hotel was another hostelry to take its name from a nearby railway. Naturally enough, its address was 1 Great Western Street.

SECTION TEN
Wednesbury People

During the 1913 Wednesbury tube strike, Brays, fish fryers, distributed free fish, donated by J.P. Johnson of Grimsby, to the oppressed locals. Pictured outside 75 to 80 Holyhead Road, the sign urges folk to 'bring your baskets'.

Cornelius Whitehouse (1795–1883) patented an improved method of tube manufacture in 1825, throwing many 'barrel forgers' out of work. Wednesbury earned the nickname 'Tubetown', but Whitehouse had to sleep with a loaded gun at his bedside.

Dr Walter Garman JP. He was Chief Medical Officer, and lived at the ancient Oakeswell Hall. His daughter, Kathleen, became the second wife of sculptor Jacob Epstein in 1955.

Historian Frederick William Hackwood JP (1851–1926), became headmaster of St Bartholomew's Schools at the tender age of twenty-one. His books about Wednesbury are now much sought after.

Undertaker Sidney Webb, 1908. He first operated from the cellar of the Talbot Hotel in 1894 before moving, first to Willow Mews, Meeting Street, then Central Mews, Upper High Street.

One of company founder Henry Hollingsworth's four sons is pictured in 1912 with apprentices Bert Williams (left) and Charles Hollingsworth (right) – his grandson – at their Holyhead Road abattoir.

Police Sergeant Lightfoot, from Wednesbury station, is pictured in the 1890s uniform of the Staffordshire constabulary.

Mary Elcock (née Danks) helped found the family firm of Elcock and Lowe Tube Works, Holyhead Road, in 1855. Their first employees' outing in 1856 was an excursion to Sutton Park. Her attire presents an excellent study of Victorian ladies' fashion.

Pictured at 14 Bridge Street, about 1900, is George Westbury (centre), with his traditional pet Staffordshire bull terrier.

Born at the Elizabethan Talbot Hotel, Market Place, in 1825, the Revd William Salter-Price, pictured here in 1900, became a church missionary in 1849, establishing the African Frere town in 1874.

Joseph Pym, keeper of Brunswick Park, strolls along the Invalids' Walk on Christmas Eve, 1902.

Lady Emily Foley (1805–1900), daughter of the third Duke and Duchess of Montrose, married the Hon. Edward Thomas Foley MP, whose seat was Stoke Edith Park in Herefordshire. Following his death on 29 March 1846, she acquired Wednesbury's manorial rights, part owned by Sir Francis Scott, Bt., of Great Barr Park.

Four Wednesbury lads pose for this rustic study in Herbert Hill's Jubilee Studio, Bridge Street, *c*. 1905.

Businessman George J. Dale plays host to a garden party in the grounds of his home, Portland House, Wood Green, *c*. 1935.

Film actress, Miss Evelyn Laye, crowned the Carnival Queen, Miss P. Thompson (seated), at the Town Hall contest, 2 September 1931. The attendants are, left to right: Lily Doleman, Lily Palmer, Vera Sale, Miriam Smith.

Pictured at the House of Commons in 1955 are members of Wednesbury Corporation's Public Health Committee. Ethel Price, twice mayor (and the only woman to hold the post), stands in the centre of the front row. To her left is Stanley Evans, Wednesbury MP, who earned the title 'featherbed' for opposing farming subsidies.

Dr Edward Alfred Dingley JP
(1860–1948) was the poor law
medical officer, who lived at
1 Loxdale Street. A keen
photographer, some of his pictures
appear on these pages.

John F. Ede, 1945. He was history master
at Wednesbury Boys' High School, and in
1962 wrote the *History of Wednesbury*,
a copy of which was presented to Queen
Elizabeth II.

Wednesbury Civil Defence ladies take charge of the pig roast at the 75th anniversary charter gala, held at Hydes Road playing fields on 8 July 1961.

Civil Defence members make a presentation of fishing tackle, c. 1966. Front row, left to right: Leslie Crouch, -?-, Frederick Clarke, -?-, Hilda Proctor.

Wednesbury Labour Club darts team with an impressive array of trophies, 1952.

Members of the Gill family get together for a social evening at the Civil Defence Club, Hawthorne Road, *c.* 1972.

SECTION ELEVEN
Streets and Buildings

Bridge Street, 1900. This picture shows the Drill Hall and adjacent sergeant instructor's house, built in 1893.

Holyhead Road, 1900. The Town Hall (left) was built in 1871 and remodelled in 1913. To its right stands the Art Gallery, bequeathed by husband and wife, Edwin and Mary Anne Richards, and built in 1891.

Central Mews, the Upper High Street premises of century-old Sidney Webb and Sons, Undertakers, 1920s. To the left, the figure of Columbia can just be discerned on the roof of the Palace cinema.

Upper High Street, 1900. This was originally part of the London to Holyhead coaching road until Thomas Telford's improvements of 1826.

Lower High Street displays its wealth of Georgian buildings, 1905. Foster Brothers clothing company display their wares on the far left.

This idyllic scene at Wood Green is now part of the busy approach road to Junction 9 of the M5. Pictured in 1912, the 'Fleam Bridge' carried the road over the mill stream to Wednesbury Forge.

Oakeswell Hall, Walsall Street, 1897. The Hall took its name from the ancient Oakes Well, which remains on the site. First mentioned in 1421, it was finally demolished in 1962.

The White Horse tram terminus, which took its name from the adjacent hotel (right), *c*. 1930. Lloyds Bank (left), was founded by Wednesbury industrialist Sampson Lloyd III (1728–1807).

Trouse Lane is seen from its junction with Wellcroft Street, *c*. 1956. On the left-hand gable, a billboard advertises the Palace cinema.

Miss Jean Nicholls cycles along the cobbled surface of High Bullen, passing the remains of James Russell's Crown Tube Works, 1952. Today, High Bullen is a busy dual carriageway.

The junction of Union Street with High Bullen, 1950. The six-sided toll house was a remnant from turnpike days.

Mr W.S. George operated these petrol pumps at his Piercy Street garage, Mesty Croft, next door to the family home, 45 Hydes Road, in 1964.

Addison Street, 1963. It was named after the Addison family, who gave the land on which St John's Church was built.

Pictured in the winter of 1988, these Moxley High Street shops were demolished in February 1992.

These Union Street shops, pictured in 1969, were demolished in the late 1970s to make way for a superstore development.

SECTION TWELVE
Royal Occasions

Carpenters under the King Edward VII coronation arch, on the Spring Head approach to the town centre, 1902.

The parish church Young Men's Social Club, 16 Market Place, is seen dressed up for the 1902 coronation celebrations.

Another patriotic display was provided at the Conservative Club's Spring Head House in Walsall Street. Lord Windsor opened a new building on the site in 1904. Note the man on the roof.

See if you can spot Edward, Prince of Wales, in the crowds assembled in Market Place during his royal visit on 13 June 1923.

Beech Road residents don their party hats in celebration of the coronation of Queen Elizabeth II, 2 June 1953.

Another coronation street party was held on 2 June by the residents of Chestnut Road on the Golflinks Estate.

The mayor, Councillor Leonard Waldron, receives Queen Elizabeth II on her royal visit to the borough, 24 May 1962.

Friar Park children enjoy Silver Jubilee festivities on 27 July 1977.

When refused a grant of road closure, the Ford family held these Silver Jubilee celebrations in the garden of 30 Manor Road, Friar Park.

Acknowledgements

The author would like to thank all the individuals and organizations listed below for either the loan of photographs or provision of information used in this book. Their kindness is sincerely appreciated.

Mabel Bailey • Anne Betteridge • Dorothy Blocksidge • Christopher Bott
David Bott • Eric Bott • Katharine Clarke • Katharine Dudley
Lilian Fairbrother • Marie Farquhar • A.T. Foley • Brian Ford
Brenda Greenhough • Brenda Griffiths • Florence Hignett • Mark Hooper
Kathleen Hudson • Mrs Ingram • Brian Jones • Doreen Knill
David Knowles • Marian Maczka • Tony Mallam • Irene Mitchell
Jeff Mitchell • Dora Palmer • Olive Parker • Robert Robson • Jocelyn Spicer
Annie Spittle • Patricia Stevenson • Sam Stevenson • Gary Talbot
Tony Turton • Carl Vaughan • Wesley Whitehouse • Connie Willetts
Cyril Willetts • Mr Wood • Black Country Society • Avril and Trevor of
Sidney Webb & Sons Ltd • Wednesbury Local History Society